WHERE HAD HE COME FROM?

They backtracked him on the north slope, which was covered with deep snow because it received little sun. Cronin worked his way down beside the tracks for several hundred yards ... the visitor had evidently strode up that declivity; his prints seemed to come from over the edge of the earth, up out of the valley far below. He must have been as strong as a gorilla, or stronger ...

THE YETI . . .
WAS HE FANTASY OR FACT,
STRANGER THAN FICTION?